THE STORY OF
FLIGHT
LIZZY PEARL

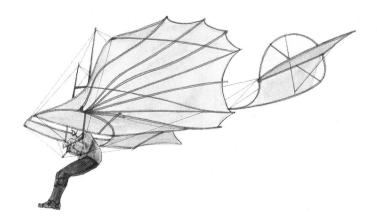

Illustrated by
MARK BERGIN

Troll Associates

Library of Congress Cataloging-in-Publication Data

Pearl, Lizzy.
 The story of flight / by Lizzy Pearl; illustrated by Mark Bergin.
  p.   cm.
 Includes index.
 Summary: Surveys the history of aviation, from the first attempts
to modern supersonic planes.
 ISBN 0-8167-2709-0 (lib. bdg.)   ISBN 0-8167-2710-4 (pbk.)
  1. Flight—History—Juvenile literature.   2. Aeronautics—History—
Juvenile literature. [1. Flight—History.   2. Aeronautics—
History. 3. Airplanes—History.] I. Bergin, Mark, ill.
II. Title.
TL547.P37 1993
629.13'009—dc20   91-33412

Published by Troll Associates

© 1994 Eagle Books

Design by James Marks
Edited by Kate Woodhouse

Printed in the U.S.A.

10 9 8 7 6 5 4 3 2 1

Contents

The dream of flight

For thousands of years people have dreamed of flying. A Greek story tells of Daedalus and his son Icarus, who made themselves wings to escape from Crete. Icarus flew too close to the sun and his wings melted. He crashed to the earth and was killed. There is another story of an ancient king of Persia called Ka'us who tied four large doves to his throne and took off.

▼ In the mid-18th century, the Marquis de Bacqueville tried to fly over the Seine River in Paris. He took off from his mansion nearby, crash-landed on a washerwoman's barge, and broke his leg.

For centuries people tried to imitate birds by strapping wings made of wood, feathers, and fabric to their backs. Many of them were badly injured or killed. The mistake they all made was to try and imitate the flight of birds. They thought that if they flapped their arms hard enough, they would be able to fly. But the muscle power of a bird's wings is much greater than a human's arms in comparison with their weights. People will never be able to fly on their own.

▲ King Ka'us of Persia flying on his bejeweled throne.

▲ The artist and inventor Leonardo da Vinci designed a flying machine called an helixpteron, the first helicopter.

5

Up, up, and away

One day the inventors hit on another idea—the balloon. The most famous balloonists were two French brothers, the Montgolfiers. They built a hot-air balloon about 35 feet (11 meters) in diameter and made it rise by burning straw under the balloon.

On November 21, 1783, two men took off in the Montgolfiers' balloon and became the first men to make a free flight. They flew for 25 minutes over Paris, watched by the excited Parisians.

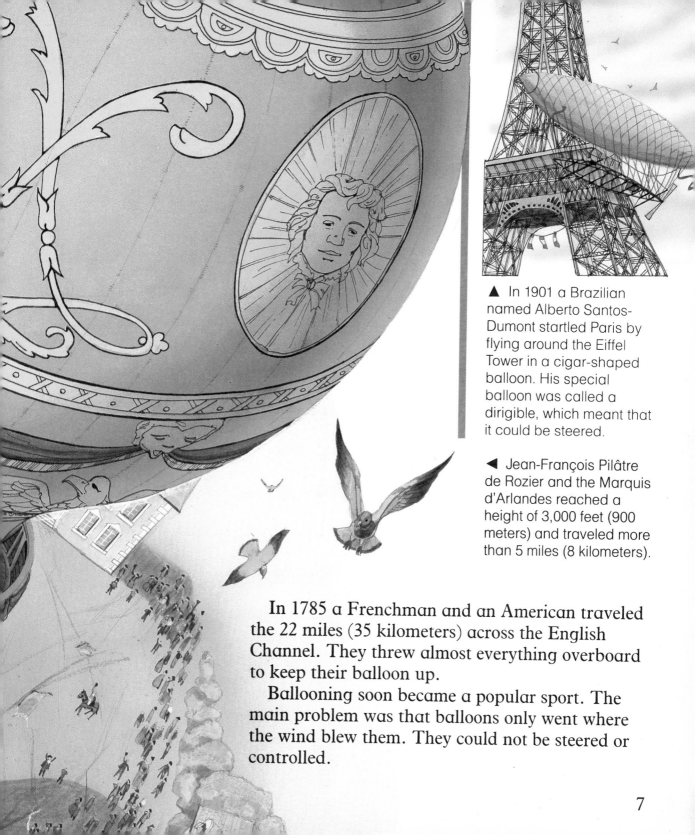

▲ In 1901 a Brazilian named Alberto Santos-Dumont startled Paris by flying around the Eiffel Tower in a cigar-shaped balloon. His special balloon was called a dirigible, which meant that it could be steered.

◄ Jean-François Pilâtre de Rozier and the Marquis d'Arlandes reached a height of 3,000 feet (900 meters) and traveled more than 5 miles (8 kilometers).

In 1785 a Frenchman and an American traveled the 22 miles (35 kilometers) across the English Channel. They threw almost everything overboard to keep their balloon up.

Ballooning soon became a popular sport. The main problem was that balloons only went where the wind blew them. They could not be steered or controlled.

First attempts

An Englishman, Sir George Cayley, is thought of as the father of aviation, the art of flying. He first experimented with kites and then began building gliders. A glider has no engine, but is kept in the air by air currents. In 1849 Cayley sent a ten-year-old boy up in a three-winged glider.

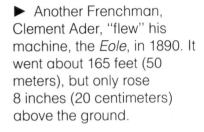

▶ Another Frenchman, Clement Ader, "flew" his machine, the *Eole*, in 1890. It went about 165 feet (50 meters), but only rose 8 inches (20 centimeters) above the ground.

▲ In 1874 a Frenchman, Félix du Temple, made the first attempt to fly a steam-powered machine. It took off from a ramp, hopped a few yards and crashed.

▶ Samuel Langley's *Aerodrome* had a gasoline engine. In 1903, it was launched from a catapult over the Potomac River and fell straight into the water.

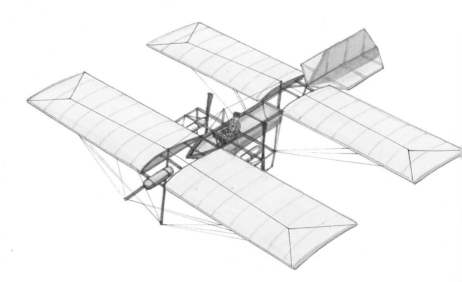

Another gliding pioneer was a German engineer, Otto Lilienthal. He made gliders of wood and waxed cloth. He made over 2,500 flights, but was killed in 1896 when his glider crashed.

Both Cayley and Lilienthal realized that a small but powerful engine was necessary to fly a plane. At that time there were only steam engines, which were too large and heavy. Some pioneers did try them, but with little success.

▲ Lilienthal controlled his flight by moving his body within the harness that supported him.

The Wright brothers

In 1903 two American brothers changed the course of history. Orville and Wilbur Wright, who ran a bicycle shop, spent their spare time building gliders. Finally they decided to build a powered airplane. They made an engine and installed it in the *Flyer*. At 10:35 A.M. on December 17, Orville Wright took off and flew the *Flyer* for 12 seconds, covering 120 feet (37 meters). It was the first successful powered flight.

▼ The *Flyer* making its historic flight, with Wilbur running alongside as Orville struggles with the controls.

That day the *Flyer* made three more flights. On the last it flew for 59 seconds and traveled more than 850 feet (260 meters). But a few minutes later, a gust of wind overturned it and wrecked it.

Sadly, few people took notice of the Wright brothers' historic flight. It was not until 1906, in Europe, that people began to take a real interest in flying. However, the Wright brothers had shown that airplanes could fly.

▲The Wrights invented a system called "wing warping," which moved part of the wings (shown in red) and gave the *Flyer* balance. The pilot lay on the bottom wing with his hips in a cradle. As he moved from side to side, the cradle pulled the wing-warping wires.

Magnificent men in their flying machines

Between 1906 and 1914 many people spent fortunes risking their lives in their flying machines. In 1906 in France, Alberto Santos-Dumont flew about 720 feet (220 meters) in his *14 bis*. In 1907 an Anglo-Frenchman, Henri Farman, made the first circular flight. Until then nobody was sure if a plane could fly in a circle.

▼ Blériot had no navigation aids, not even a compass, when he crossed the English Channel. There was a thick mist and he had no landmarks to guide him. Even so, after 37 minutes he landed safely at Dover.

In 1908 a $2,500 prize was offered to the first person to fly across the English Channel. In 1909 an American, Hubert Latham, made the attempt, but his engine failed and he had to be rescued from the sea. On July 25, 1909, a Frenchman, Louis Blériot, was finally successful. This flight proved that airplanes could travel long distances. Now many more people wanted airplanes.

At the Rheims airshow in 1909, 250,000 people saw the latest designs and watched leading pilots compete in the first air races.

▲ The Brazilian airship-builder Alberto Santos-Dumont caused a sensation with his historic first flight in *14 bis*.

The dream becomes a nightmare

In August 1914 the First World War began. Early in the war, airplanes were used for taking photographs and sending messages. These planes were often attacked from the ground, so the pilots began to arm themselves. At first they carried handguns and fired at the enemy over the sides of their cockpits. Later they dropped bricks, grenades, or homemade bombs.

▼ Any pilot who shot down five or more planes was called an "ace." The most famous ace was Germany's Baron Manfred von Richthofen, who shot down 80 enemy planes. Here, in his scarlet Fokker, he engages in a dogfight with a British Sopwith Camel.

In 1915 the Germans developed the Fokker, which had a machine gun that could fire bullets between revolving propeller blades. Great Britain and France developed similar machines, and the skies filled with furious dogfights.

The war was a terrible period, but it helped the development of aviation. By the end of the war in 1918 thousands of people were involved in improving flying and making it safer.

The trailblazers

▼ During Lindbergh's 33½-hour flight, his greatest enemy was exhaustion. Falling asleep would have been fatal.

During the next few years, many former wartime pilots made hazardous, record-breaking flights. In 1919 two Englishmen, John Alcock and Arthur Whitten Brown, were the first to cross the Atlantic. They took off from Newfoundland in a Vickers Vimy bomber and landed in Ireland 16 hours and 27 minutes later.

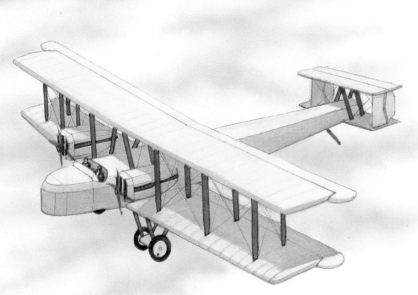

▲ Alcock and Brown flew in an open cockpit, their hands freezing. Brown had to climb onto the wing several times to hack away at ice clogging the engine.

▲ In 1928 Amelia Earhart became the first woman to fly solo across the Atlantic. In 1937 she set out to fly around the world, but her plane disappeared over the Pacific Ocean.

In May 1927 an American, Charles Lindbergh, made the first solo flight across the Atlantic. He flew nonstop from New York to Paris in his monoplane, *Spirit of St. Louis*.

Other pioneers included the Englishman Sir Alan Cobham, who mapped out all the landing places between Cairo, Egypt and Cape Town, South Africa, and between London and Melbourne, Australia. In 1928 the Australians Charles Kingsford-Smith and Charles Ulm made the first flight across the Pacific Ocean.

Over the next ten years almost every major air route was opened up by brave trailblazers.

The skies open

In 1919 the first international passenger airline service flew people daily from London to Paris. Only two or three passengers could travel at a time and it was uncomfortable. In America, airplanes only carried mail until 1927, but after Lindbergh's flight, everyone wanted to fly. Within two years America had the world's largest airline fleet, with about 15 passengers on each flight.

▼ The Boeing 247 (*top*) was the first all-metal streamlined airliner. It was followed by the Douglas DC-3 (*bottom*), which is still flying today.

Flights still took a long time. Flying from England to India took a whole week! This was because passenger aircraft were biplanes (with two sets of wings). No one had yet designed a monoplane (with one set of wings) strong enough to carry passengers and their luggage.

In 1933 the Boeing company designed the 247, the first streamlined monoplane. Its smooth, even shape gave the least resistance to movement through the air. This strong, fast aircraft revolutionized air travel.

▲ The first passengers were given a leather coat, helmet, goggles, and gloves, as well as a hot-water bottle on really cold days.

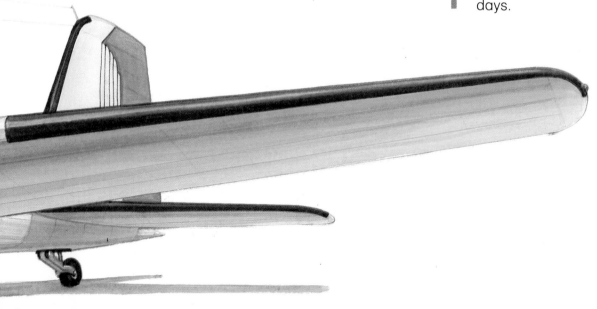

Battle for the skies

The Second World War (1939-45) saw major developments in aviation. Fighter planes became faster, and bombers were able to carry tons of explosives thousands of miles.

The first practical radar system was another great step forward. It enabled the British to detect aircraft of the German air force over 75 miles (120 kilometers) away. It was developed by a Scottish engineer, Robert Watson-Watt, and was soon used by all aircraft as an aid to navigation.

▼The Battle of Britain in 1940 was one of the most famous air battles. British fighters succeeded in preventing an invasion of Great Britain by the German forces.

Another important development was the jet engine. It was invented by a British Royal Air Force officer named Frank Whittle and was first used in 1941 to power Gloster Meteor fighters. At the same time, the Germans were developing their own jet warplanes and rockets. Their jet, the Heinkel 778, made its first flight in 1939.

◄ British Spitfires and Hurricanes fought off German Messerschmitts, Dorniers *(left)* and Junkers Ju-87 Stuka dive bombers.

► The Gloster Meteor (*bottom right*) was the only jet the British had. The German jets were the Messerschmitt Me-262 (*right*) and the Heinkel He-162 fighters. The German V-1 "doodlebug" was a jet-powered flying bomb. It was used mainly to bombard London.

21

From Comet to jumbo jet

The first jet passenger airliner was built by the de Havilland company of Great Britain and went into service in 1952. They named it the Comet. But the aircraft's metal was not strong enough, and several Comets broke up in midflight, killing all the passengers. Other manufacturers learned from these disasters and built their jets with stronger metal. The most successful were the Boeing 707 and the Douglas DC-8.

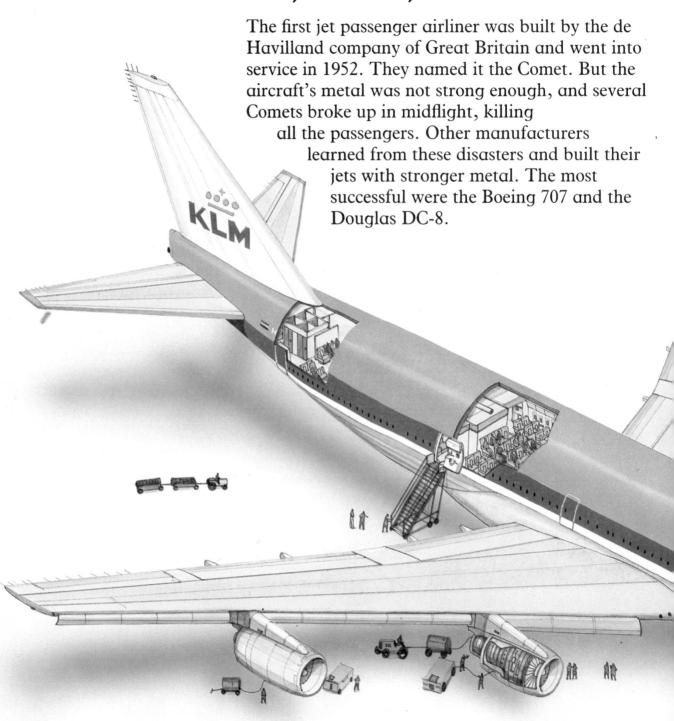

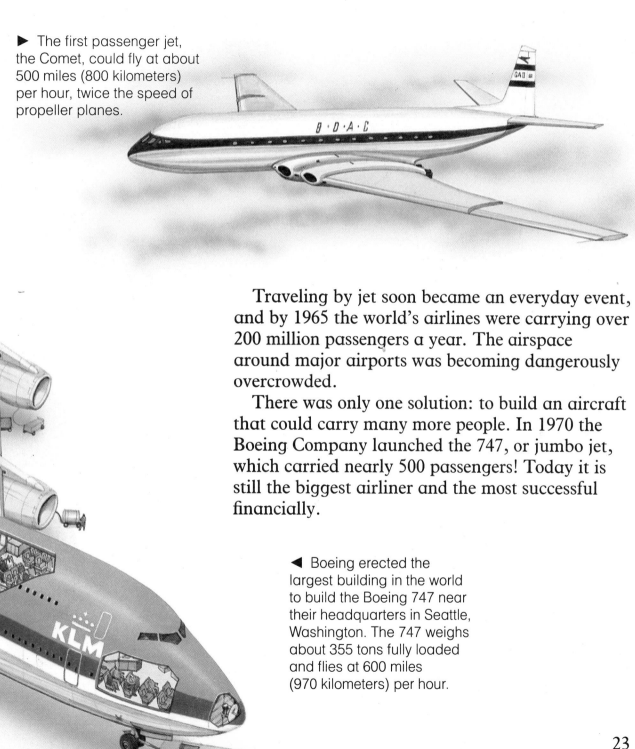

▶ The first passenger jet, the Comet, could fly at about 500 miles (800 kilometers) per hour, twice the speed of propeller planes.

Traveling by jet soon became an everyday event, and by 1965 the world's airlines were carrying over 200 million passengers a year. The airspace around major airports was becoming dangerously overcrowded.

There was only one solution: to build an aircraft that could carry many more people. In 1970 the Boeing Company launched the 747, or jumbo jet, which carried nearly 500 passengers! Today it is still the biggest airliner and the most successful financially.

◀ Boeing erected the largest building in the world to build the Boeing 747 near their headquarters in Seattle, Washington. The 747 weighs about 355 tons fully loaded and flies at 600 miles (970 kilometers) per hour.

The supersonic age

During the Second World War, pilots flying at top speed noticed that their aircraft would suddenly begin to shudder violently. This was because they were approaching the speed of sound, about 660 miles (1,060 kilometers) per hour. The speed of sound, measured in Mach numbers, is known as Mach 1. Flying slower than the speed of sound is subsonic flight. Flying faster is supersonic flight. No one knew if it was possible to fly supersonically until 1947, when a rocket-powered aircraft called the Bell X-1 was flown at Mach 1.05. It was the first supersonic flight.

The Bell X program developed even faster aircraft. In 1959 the X-15 flew at Mach 6.5 – six-and-a-half times the speed of sound! Then, in 1969, the world watched as the Anglo-French supersonic aircraft, the Concorde, made its first flight. The Concorde is still the only supersonic passenger airline service in the world.

▶ The Concorde can cross the Atlantic in less than three hours, flying at Mach 2.2 (over twice the speed of sound). Only sixteen Concordes have been built.

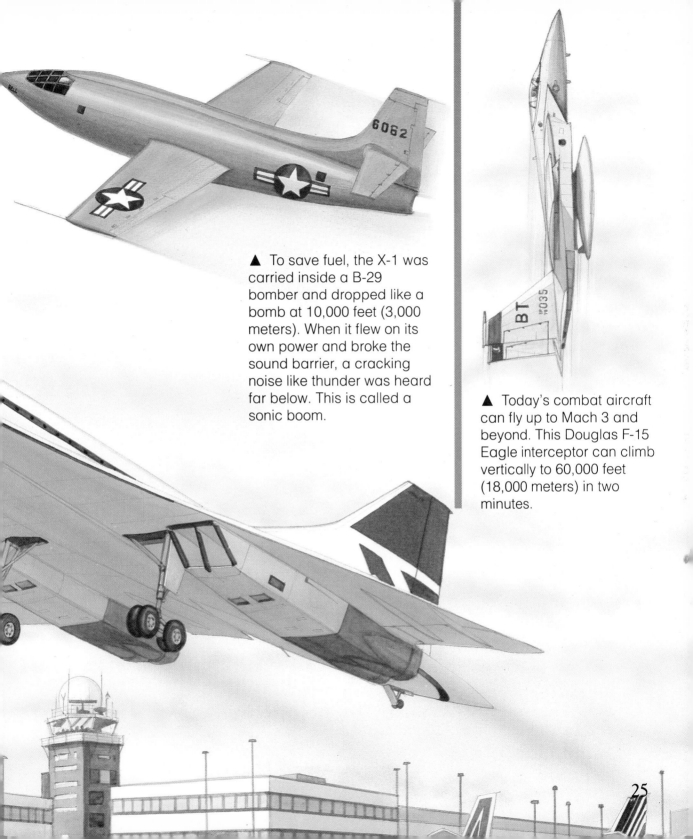

▲ To save fuel, the X-1 was carried inside a B-29 bomber and dropped like a bomb at 10,000 feet (3,000 meters). When it flew on its own power and broke the sound barrier, a cracking noise like thunder was heard far below. This is called a sonic boom.

▲ Today's combat aircraft can fly up to Mach 3 and beyond. This Douglas F-15 Eagle interceptor can climb vertically to 60,000 feet (18,000 meters) in two minutes.

Different planes for different jobs

Since the Wright brothers' flight in 1903, aircraft have become such a part of everyday life that it is difficult to imagine a world without them. Aircraft are not only used for passenger travel and military purposes. They have many other uses: freight, rescue, medical supply, farming, observation, and research.

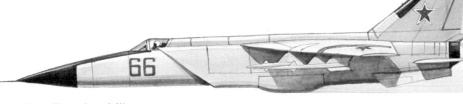

▲ This Russian Mikoyan MiG25 "Foxbat" is the fastest fighter in the world. It flies at Mach 3.2.

◀ Helicopters are used in a wide range of activities: spraying crops, spotting traffic jams, rescuing people at sea, and policing. They are also used to rescue the injured in wartime, and to carry soldiers to and from places where an airplane cannot land. This Boeing Chinook is so strong it can lift a personnel carrier.

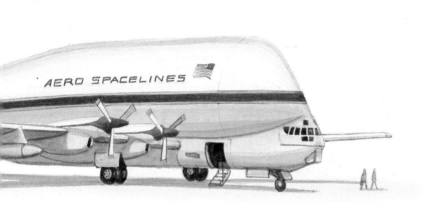

▲ The Super Guppy is the world's largest aircraft and can carry weights up to 80 tons. It is used to carry huge pieces of equipment such as rocket parts.

▲ The Rolls-Royce "Flying Bedstead" was used for experiments with vertical takeoff and landing. Its jets were powered downward so it took off upward.

XV788

▲ Britain's Hawker Siddeley Harrier jump jet can rise vertically from an area little more than its own size and then fly supersonically.

Into the future

The Wright brothers would have found it difficult to imagine the aircraft of today. Computer technology means that flying may soon be fully automated. All the pilot will have to do is set the controls. Planes will be made of light plastic or carbon fiber, and one day some might be nuclear powered. Whatever the future of aviation brings, it is bound to be as exciting as its past.

▶ This is the latest American warplane. Code-named Aurora, this 90-foot (30-meter) "flying dart" can be an unmanned aircraft, a bomber, or a spy plane. It will reach Mach 6 and no missile will be able to catch it.

▶ The Interim HOTOL (Horizontal Takeoff and Landing) reusable space vehicle will be launched from an aircraft.

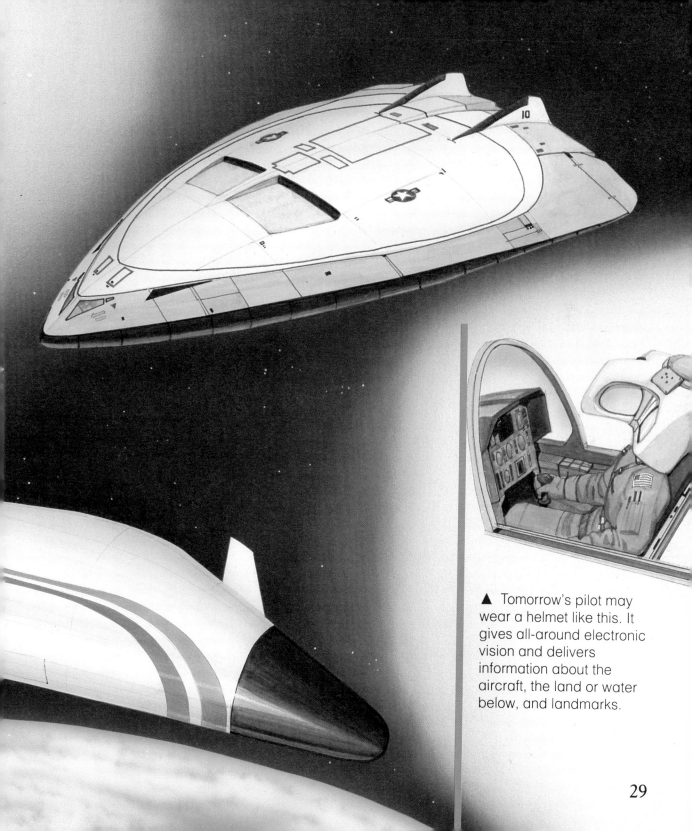

▲ Tomorrow's pilot may wear a helmet like this. It gives all-around electronic vision and delivers information about the aircraft, the land or water below, and landmarks.

Fact file

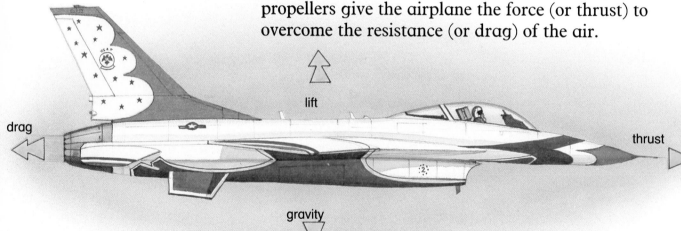

Air moving over curved wing

▲ The air flowing over the curved wing is going faster than the air below it. The pressure above the wing is less than the pressure below it, which causes the wing to rise.

drag

lift

thrust

gravity

How a plane flies

If you look closely at the wing of an aircraft, you will see that the top edge is curved more than the bottom. This is because air flows faster over a curved surface. As it does, the pressure above the wing lessens, which causes the wing to rise. This is called lift.

When a plane flies, there are four forces acting on it: lift, gravity, thrust, and drag. The lift of the wings has to overcome the downward pull of the airplane's weight if the plane is to rise. The jets or propellers give the airplane the force (or thrust) to overcome the resistance (or drag) of the air.

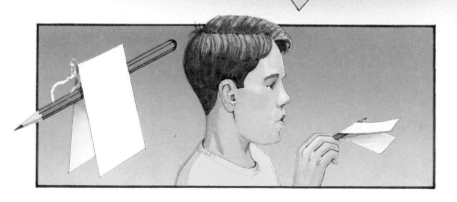

◀ To understand lift, fold a piece of paper in half and rest it along a pencil. Blow along the length of the pencil. You might expect the paper to move along the pencil. Instead it rises. Its "airfoil" shape acts just like a wing.

How a jet engine works

Jet engines suck air in at one end and force it out at the other end at much greater speed. After the air is sucked in, part of it is mixed with ignited fuel, which produces hot gases. The heated gases expand and take up space. These gases can go out only through the back of the engine. As jets of gas shoot backward, the engine is thrust forward.

▲ To see how a jet engine works, blow up a balloon. Then let the balloon go. The air escaping backward pushes the balloon forward.

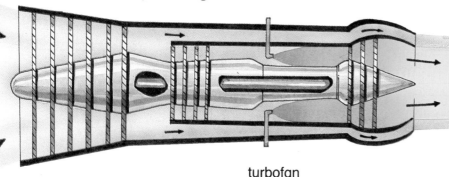

turbofan

▲ The turbofan has a fan and compressor at the front to suck in air. It sucks in about fives times as much air as is needed to burn the fuel. The excess air mixes with the exhaust gases to cool the engine. Today's airliners have up to four turbofans.

▼ Turbojets are smaller and less powerful than turbofans, but they can be fitted with afterburners, which re-explode the gases at the back of the engine to increase the thrust.

▼ Turboprops act just like turbojets, but their turbines also drive a propeller. They are popular for transporting heavy cargo.

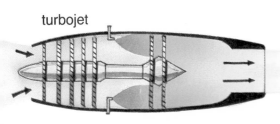

turbojet

turboprop

31

Index